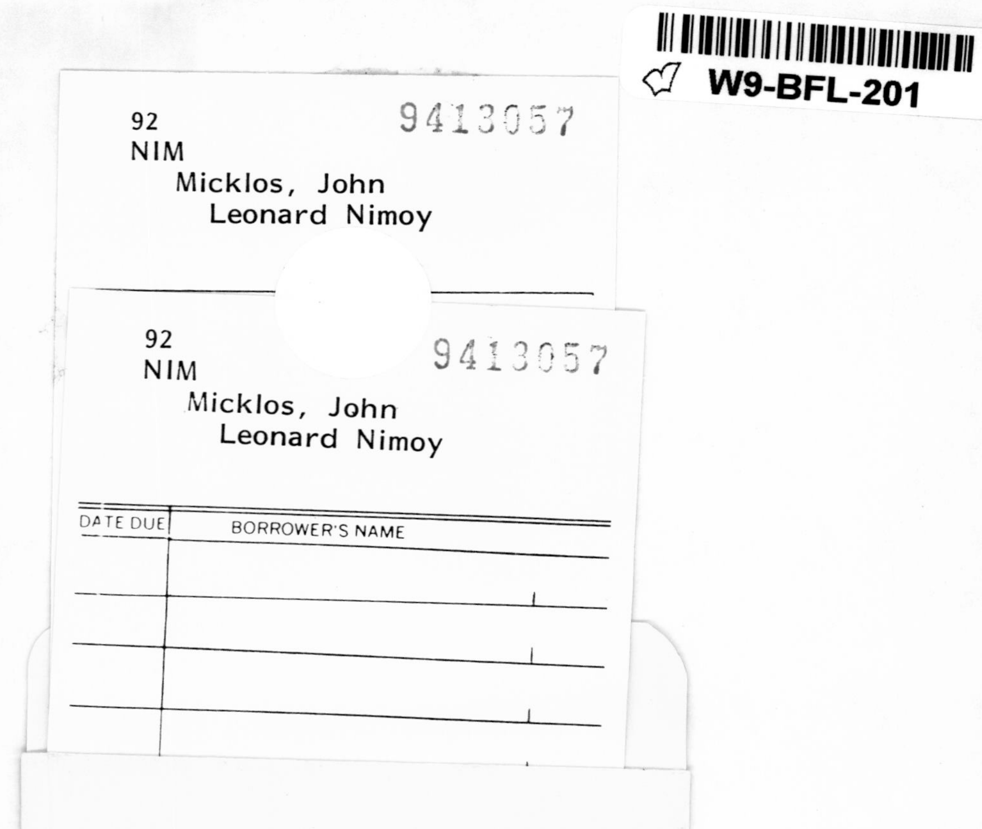
92
NIM
9413057
Micklos, John
Leonard Nimoy
92
NIM
9413057
Micklos, John
Leonard Nimoy
DATE DUE
BORROWER'S NAME

LEONARD NIMOY

★ A STAR'S TREK ★

JOHN MICKLOS, JR.

Dillon Press
New York

Collier Macmillan Canada
Toronto

Maxwell Macmillan International Publishing Group
New York Oxford Singapore Sydney

Photographic Acknowledgments

Photographs have been reproduced through the courtesy of Dennis Babcock; © Fotos International (pages 24, 28, 32, 50); © Fotos International/Frank Edwards (pages 19, 21, 53); Globe Photos/Bob Noble; Globe Photos/Ralph Dominguez (cover); Henry Grossman; London Features International/Kevin Mazur; and Greg Schwartz.

Library of Congress Cataloging-in-Publication Data

Micklos, John, Jr.
Leonard Nimoy : a star's trek / by John Micklos, Jr.
p. cm. — (Taking part books)
Includes index.
SUMMARY: Examines the life of the actor who became popular as Mr. Spock on the television series "Star Trek" and later branched out into writing poetry and directing some of the Star Trek films.
ISBN 0-87518-376-X
1. Nimoy, Leonard—Juvenile literature. 2. Authors, American—20th century—Biography—Juvenile literature. 3. Motion picture actors and actresses—United States—Biography--Juvenile literature. [1. Nimoy, Leonard. 2. Actors and actresses. 3. Motion picture producers and directors.] I. Title.

PS3564.I5Z78 1988
791.45'028'0924—dc19
[B]
[92]

87-32457
CIP
AC

Macmillan Publishing Company, 866 Third Avenue
New York, NY 10022

Printed in the United States of America
2 3 4 5 6 7 8 9 10

★ CONTENTS ★

★ *Leonard Nimoy* ★

Leonard Nimoy—better known as "Star Trek's" Mr. Spock—has loved acting since he was a small child in Boston, Massachusetts, during the 1930s. In time, he knew he wanted to be a serious actor. Against the wishes of his parents, he packed up and headed for Hollywood, California.

After playing roles in television shows such as "Gunsmoke" and "Dragnet," Nimoy's career skyrocketed when he agreed to play the likable, logical Mr. Spock on the science fiction series, "Star Trek." Years later he agreed to put his Spock ears back on and act in the "Star Trek" movies. As a tribute to his many years of acting in Hollywood, Leonard Nimoy has earned his own star on the Hollywood Walk of Fame.

Acting is not Nimoy's only talent. He has also directed two of the "Star Trek" movies and other recent popular films. A skillful writer and photographer, he has written six poetry books and his autobiography. Nimoy is a man of many interests, ideas, and goals. The world has not seen the last of Leonard Nimoy—or of Mr. Spock.

1

On the Outside

Leonard Nimoy has always had a soft spot for people who are a little bit different. As a boy, he cried when he saw the movie *The Hunchback of Notre Dame* because he thought people should not treat the hunchbacked man so badly. He liked Frankenstein and other monsters and aliens. Leonard knew that most people were afraid of them, but he also thought that these creatures had feelings, too. He understood.

Leonard was born on March 26, 1931, in Boston, Massachusetts. He had one older brother named Melvin. His parents, Max and Dora Nimoy, grew up together in a poor part of the Russian countryside. They were Jewish, and life was difficult for Jews in Russia at that time. The Nimoys decided to come to

America in search of a better life, and settled in Boston.

The Nimoys' Jewish roots played an important part in their lives. Leonard learned to speak Yiddish, a language spoken mainly by Eastern European Jews. Because Leonard was Jewish, he sometimes felt out of place with his friends. His neighborhood in Boston's West End was full of Catholic Italian families. "Our friendships stopped abruptly at the door of the church," he said. Leonard always seemed to feel a bit "on the outside."

Times weren't easy in America for the Nimoy family. The 1930s were the years of the Great Depression, a time when money, supplies, and jobs were scarce. Max Nimoy, Leonard's father, worked in a barber shop at first, and later became a partner in the business.

The family managed to make ends meet on his salary. Leonard tried to do his part to help out—he

Leonard and his father, Max Nimoy.

was always inventing ways to make money. His mother said that he earned his own money from the time he was eleven years old.

Leonard had many interests and hobbies to keep himself busy. He loved to take pictures, and even learned to develop his own prints. He set up a "dark-room" in the bathroom of his family's home. For him it was like magic to see the prints develop.

As a teenager, Leonard took his camera around the neighborhood. He asked if he could take pictures of the neighbors' children, and would then sell the prints to the parents. He not only earned some money, but he had the chance to practice his photography.

His mother says that he was a good boy, but didn't like to study as much as his brother Melvin. Leonard liked to spend his spare time playing in the neighborhood, watching movies, and acting in local plays. Leonard started acting when he was eight years old, playing the lead role in a local production of "Hansel and Gretel."

Leonard loved the theater. He would hang around the playhouse day and night, even if he wasn't in the performance. When he was seventeen, he had a role that was very special to him. He played Ralphie Berger in a play called "Awake and Sing" at the Elizabeth Peabody Playhouse in Boston.

Like Leonard, Ralphie was a teenager in a Jewish family during the depression. In the play, Ralphie struggles with his strong-willed mother—he wants to make his own decisions without her help. Leonard could relate to this role. His own mother was more forceful than his easygoing father.

Leonard often struggled with his parents because they never quite understood his love for acting. They were worried that being an actor wasn't the practical

Leonard and his parents, Dora and Max Nimoy, laugh together at a party.

thing for him to do. Since acting roles can be hard to come by, Leonard's parents warned him that an acting job might be risky.

Still, as time went on, Leonard wanted more and more to become an actor. A director at the Elizabeth Peabody Playhouse noticed Leonard's talent and determination, and recommended him for a scholarship in drama to Boston College. Nimoy studied acting at this college for only a few months and then dropped out. He decided that he would have a better chance to become an actor in California.

Even though his parents tried to talk him out of it, Leonard had made his decision. He took six hundred dollars that he had earned selling vacuum cleaners and took a train out west. During the three-day train trip, Leonard ate a lot of junk food, and thought about his new life in California. He was ready to be an actor, but it wasn't going to be easy.

Leonard, in the early days of his acting career.

2

Hollywood Bound

Hollywood, California, in the 1950s, was the movie-making center of the world. Actor Marlon Brando was the hit of Hollywood at that time—the typical "tough guy" who wore jeans and a T-shirt. Leonard wanted to look tough, too, so he dressed like the tough guy actors.

Leonard knew it would be hard to "break in" as an actor. He enrolled as a student at the Pasadena Playhouse while struggling to get small parts in movies and television shows. His first film role was in the movie *Queen for a Day*. He remembers the first time he saw himself on film; "I was in a state of shock for weeks," he said. Up on the screen, he saw himself as a "strange, skinny figure."

Later, a friend of Leonard's earned a role in a western film called *Dallas*. Through her, he got a chance to try out for this film. At first, the producer promised to give Nimoy a screen test, a brief film clip that shows what an actor looks like on the screen. Leonard was excited—even if he didn't get the role, he could show the screen test to other people who were hiring actors.

Leonard waited anxiously for the producer to contact him. At last, he was called into the studio. But instead of a screen test, he was only given the chance to do a short reading for the role.

Later, Leonard heard that the part had been given to someone else. Very disappointed, Leonard tried to call the producer to get him to change his mind. He was a very determined, stubborn young man, and he wasn't about to give up.

The producer didn't return his calls, so Leonard

went to his office and waited for him to come out. When the producer threatened to call the police, Leonard had no choice but to leave.

He kept working hard to find good acting roles. Finally, he got his first big break in show business. In 1952, twenty-one-year-old Nimoy played the lead role in a movie called *Kid Monk Baroni*.

The story was about an Italian boxer from New York who was born with a strangely disfigured face. To play this role, Leonard had to wear heavy foam-rubber makeup. "I found a home behind that make-up," he said. "I was much more confident and comfortable than I would have been had I been told to play a 'handsome young man'. . . . I was playing a character outside of the social mainstream—separate, unequal, alien." Leonard enjoyed acting the part of characters who were "on the outside."

He hoped that his starring role in *Kid Monk*

Baroni would lead to other big parts, but things didn't work out that way. He continued to struggle. While working at the Pasadena Playhouse, Leonard met an actress named Sandi Zober. In 1954, they were married.

Soon after the marriage, Leonard was drafted into the army. He and Sandi spent a year and a half at an army base in Fort McPherson, in Georgia. Leonard wrote and narrated shows for Special Services, a group that organized entertainment for the troops. He also worked with a theater group in nearby Atlanta in his spare time. While Leonard and Sandi were in Georgia, their first child was born. They named their daughter Julie.

Not long after Leonard's family moved back to Los Angeles, their son, Adam, was born. Leonard couldn't be with Sandi on the day of Adam's birth, because he was in New York State working on a

Sandi and Leonard at the 1968 Emmy nominations.

television role. Good acting jobs were few and far between for Leonard, and he often had to travel with his work.

Times were hard at first for Leonard's family. He couldn't support them on his acting income alone, and had to take a number of odd jobs to make ends meet. He opened a pet shop and worked in a soda fountain, delivered newspapers, drove cabs, and ran a vending machine route.

Sandi remembered these times well. "Leonard wasn't much fun in those days, and I didn't always appreciate what a strong husband and father he was. But we worked things through," she said. Sandi wanted him to continue his acting because she knew that it was his dream to become a well-known actor.

In 1958, Leonard began to study acting with Jeff Corey in Hollywood. After two years, Corey asked Nimoy to help him teach. Leonard did this for two

Standing in front of Leonard Nimoy's Pet Pad, Leonard and an elephant draw quite a crowd.

more years, and then opened up his own studio to teach acting.

Leonard enjoyed teaching. One of his favorite acting techniques was using costumes, makeup, and disguises to make the actor feel more like the character being played. For example, dressing up in a long, sweeping cape could help an actor feel like a dashing prince. Leonard himself often used clothing and stage makeup to feel more comfortable with his acting roles.

In the early 1960s, Leonard had a major role in the play "Deathwatch." He played a French criminal who was in jail. This character didn't get along with other people—even his fellow inmates didn't like him. The critics thought that Nimoy played the role well, and Leonard decided to help produce a film version of "Deathwatch."

Bit by bit, Leonard began to get bigger and better roles. He appeared in plays, movies, and many popular TV shows such as "Gunsmoke," "Bonanza," "Dr. Kildare," "Rawhide," and "Dragnet." His acting career at last seemed a little more secure.

In 1965, Leonard had a guest-starring role on the NBC show, "The Lieutenant," an adventure series about the Marine Corps. Gene Roddenberry, the producer of that show, was also making plans to do a science fiction series called "Star Trek."

Roddenberry wanted one of the stars of the show to be an alien named Mr. Spock. He knew right away that Nimoy would be right for this role. In fact, he created the character with him in mind. Roddenberry tried to talk him into acting the part of Spock.

Leonard was thrilled with the thought of being a regular in a TV series. Nearly all actors want this type of work because it provides a steady income for as long as the show lasts. For a struggling actor, such an offer is a dream come true. Nimoy also liked the idea of playing an alien. In the end, he decided to join the "Star Trek" crew.

Mr. Spock became Leonard Nimoy's most famous acting role.

3

Mr. Spock

"To explore strange new worlds. To seek out new life and new civilizations. To boldly go where no man has gone before."

This was the mission of the Starship *Enterprise*, which made its first "Star Trek" flight on September 8, 1966. Viewers got their first glimpse of Mr. Spock, the half-human, half-alien being from the planet Vulcan.

With his pointed ears and slanting eyebrows, Spock looked quite different from any other major character on TV. The special effects crew took a long time to design Spock's ears. NBC was concerned about the pointed ears because the network thought they made Spock look like the devil!

The other cast members often made jokes about the pointed ears. At one point, Leonard asked that the ears be removed. He feared they made Spock look silly. Producer Gene Roddenberry asked that he wear them for the first thirteen shows. He promised an "ear job" if Nimoy still did not like the ears by that time. The ears became Spock's trademark, though, and he never did have the "ear job." In fact, for many years Leonard kept a set of Spock's ears mounted in his home.

Roddenberry and Nimoy worked hard to make Mr. Spock's character a strong one. They talked about Spock's background, what Spock's home planet of Vulcan would be like, and Spock's parents. Leonard has said that the process of creating this new "being" was like giving birth.

Leonard did a lot on his own to develop the character of Spock. At first, Spock was "all brain and no heart"—he was completely logical. But Nimoy saw more possibilities for Spock. He fought for lines and stories that would make Spock more interesting—and more human. Fans love seeing the rare times when Spock shows his "human side."

As the series went on, fans grew used to Spock's special traits. For instance, he sometimes raises a single eyebrow to show that he is interested or puzzled. When one of the human crew members expresses strong emotions, or feelings, Spock calmly notes, "That is illogical." Fans also enjoy watching Spock use the Vulcan neck pinch, an action that knocks a person out without doing any real harm.

On the show, Spock and his crewmates find themselves involved in adventures all over the galaxy. They face many dangers and meet all sorts of strange beings. They often fight with their enemies, the Klingons and the Romulans.

The "Star Trek" crew, including Sulu, McCoy, Kirk, Spock, and Scott, takes on another adventure.

Since "Star Trek" is a science fiction series, viewers have learned many new terms such as "phasers," "beam me up," "warp drive," and "mind melds." Sometimes viewers want to know how the special effects are created, such as how people "beam up" to the ship. Nimoy says that this is done through a simple technique called "film dissolve." Film is first shot in the empty transporter, and then with the person inside. Overlapping the film gives the effect of a person "beaming up." Special effects people then add some "sprinkles."

Fans like the action and the characters of "Star Trek." As science officer, Mr. Spock is in the midst of it all. Captain Kirk (played by William Shatner) can always count on Spock's logic and loyalty. Nurse Christine Chapel (played by Majel Barrett) has a crush on him, but he does not return her love. Some of Spock's finest moments come as a part of his friendly "feud" with the ship's doctor, McCoy (played by DeForest Kelley).

Spock soon became a hero to viewers. "Star Trek" fan clubs formed all over the country, and some of them were just for Spock. Many people also began giving each other the Vulcan salute, "Live long and prosper." Along with the phrase goes a V-shaped hand signal. The thumb is stretched out while the second and third fingers, and the fourth and fifth fingers, are held together. Nimoy says that he adapted this hand signal from a Jewish greeting.

The "Star Trek" fans were loyal to the show. When NBC tried to cancel it after two years, they sent in over 100,000 pieces of mail asking that it remain on the air. NBC finally agreed to renew the show, but the network changed the schedule of "Star Trek" to ten o'clock on Friday nights. Since the late time slot made it hard for the show's many young fans to watch it, "Star Trek" was canceled after three years. Leonard was not upset when the show was taken off the air. He felt that it was not as good in its third year as it had been before. In fact, he had often thought of quitting.

He was amazed at how closely he became linked with Spock in those three years on television. What started out as "a welcome job for a hungry actor" turned into a role that will always be remembered. Nimoy was nominated for three Emmy awards for playing Spock. He recalls that he and his wife cried when they found out about the first nomination. Though he never won the award, they were happy and excited.

All in all, Leonard enjoys his role as Spock. He has said that if he could choose to be any TV character ever played, he would take Spock. "I like him," said Leonard. "I admire him. I respect him."

Mr. Spock, at the Enterprise *control panel.*

Fans sometimes want to know if Nimoy is like Spock. In some ways he is. Like Spock, Leonard thinks it is important to be logical. He is quiet and serious, and some people say he is intense. Leonard, unlike Spock, is not afraid to show his feelings—people have described him as warm and friendly.

Leonard is an ambitious actor, and he takes his work very seriously. "Right or wrong, drama is for me a kind of spiritual crusade," he said. By "spiritual crusade" he means that acting is more than a job for him. Being the best actor he can be means a great deal to him as a person. He put a lot of effort and creative energy into his role as Mr. Spock—with the same intense determination that he puts into every role he plays.

After "Star Trek" was over, Leonard was ready to move on to new projects. But he would find that it was not so easy to leave Mr. Spock behind him.

Leonard loves all kinds of animals—once he had a dog named Spock!

4

Life Was Never Dull

When Leonard finished filming "Star Trek," he wasn't sure what he would do next. But Paramount Pictures, the makers of "Star Trek," had some ideas. Paramount was in charge of the popular adventure show, "Mission: Impossible." One of the stars of this program had just quit, and the producers asked Nimoy if he would be interested in joining the cast.

Though Leonard wasn't sure that he wanted to jump right back into another series, he liked the idea of playing "Paris," a master of disguise. The role would allow him to play many types of characters—he could be the "man of a thousand faces." Nimoy, after acting in a few shows on a trial basis, agreed to sign a four-year contract.

"Mission: Impossible" was fun for Leonard—for a while. He enjoyed wearing all of the different costumes. Sometimes his disguises were so good that the audience didn't even know the character was Leonard! During the second year of "Mission: Impossible," he began to have his doubts about his role. He became bored with it, because he couldn't develop the character of Paris like he could with Spock. Since playing Paris was no longer a challenge for him, he asked to be released from his contract.

Though the producers were sorry to see Nimoy go, they did not stand in his way. "Mission: Impossible" continued to do well for a few more years. Leonard knew that he was taking a risk in leaving this show, but he was not worried. By this time he had plenty of money to live comfortably with his family—at least for a year or two. He felt that he needed a change.

Leonard was ready to take a break from acting. He wanted some time to himself to devote to his own interests and hobbies—and some time to spend with his family. Back in his two-story house on the West Side of Los Angeles, Leonard took up gardening and photography. He bought new camera equipment and set up a darkroom in his house.

Although he enjoyed having the time to be creative, his "break" didn't last long. One day when he was developing photographs in his darkroom, the phone rang. He was asked to costar in a western called *Catlow*, to be released in 1971. This was his first movie offer in many years. Leonard accepted, partly because the movie would be filmed in Spain. He would be able to take some good pictures, and it would make a nice trip for his wife and children.

Just before he left for Spain, Leonard heard about

a part in a musical that interested him. The role was that of Tevye in "Fiddler on the Roof." This musical was about a Jewish family that leaves Russia to go to America—just as the Nimoys had done before Leonard was born. "Their story was the story of my own family," said Leonard.

Leonard asked to try out for the part. The producer did not know if Nimoy would be right for the role, but Leonard convinced him that he was. He carried the script with him to Spain, and studied it as he sat on the beach during breaks in the filming of *Catlow*. He even taped the music of "Fiddler on the Roof," so that he could learn the songs.

Fortunately, Nimoy's role in *Catlow* was small, so he had plenty of time to roam around Spain taking pictures. Just as he did when he was a child in Boston, he locked himself in the hotel's bathroom to develop his photographs.

Almost as soon as he returned from Spain, Leonard started work in the play "Fiddler on the Roof." Leonard really enjoyed the role. He has said that he had the feeling of "knowing what I was doing and why I was doing it."

One night when he was warming up with the piano for his opening song, he noticed a crowd of actors, dancers, and singers coming into the room. Someone stepped forward and handed Leonard a box wrapped up in a ribbon. When Leonard opened the gift, he found a beautiful pair of candelabras, traditional Jewish candlestick holders. Leonard was deeply moved, and the "Fiddler on the Roof" crew cried tears of happiness with him. For Leonard, playing in this production was one of the greatest experiences of his life.

Leonard kept busy acting in plays and musicals throughout the United States. Nimoy portrayed many types of characters such as the evil Fagin in "Oliver," and King Arthur in "Camelot." This kind of acting didn't pay very well, but the money wasn't that important to him. He was acting for the love of it.

Nimoy toured cities all over the country, and his family often went with him. Being on the road didn't seem to affect the educations of Julie and Adam. Both went to college and went on to have their own careers. Julie was an art major at the University of California in Santa Barbara, and later became a make-up artist. Leonard's son Adam went on from his studies as a political science major at the University of California, Berkeley, to become a lawyer.

Leonard was very busy with his "on the road" acting career, but he also found time to pursue his own interests. He was active in politics, and he learned to play the guitar, compose songs, and fly a plane. Leonard even went back to college at age

The Nimoy family makes a rare appearance in 1967 at Hollywood's annual Santa Claus parade. Leonard stands with Julie, Adam, and Sandi.

One of Leonard's favorite pastimes was gardening in his California home.

forty-four. Life was never dull for Leonard because he continued to challenge himself. He wrote six poetry books, including a book called *You and I* which contained some of his poetry and photographs.

Writing was a new experience for Leonard. In acting, he was always using someone else's words—he was memorizing lines. Now, he was using his own words, and showing the public what he himself was like. This was a bit difficult for Leonard, who is a very private person. He said that ". . .getting into writing is suddenly a very dangerous and scary experience because it is personal and it is real."

In 1975, Leonard wrote his autobiography, a story of his own life. He called it *I Am Not Spock*. That title seemed fitting, because no matter what he did, people still thought of him as the green-blooded Vulcan Spock. Leonard could use this to his advantage. "Star Trek" fans often invited Nimoy to be the guest speaker at colleges and conventions. Leonard also created some albums with the "Spock" theme, including *Leonard Nimoy Presents: Mr. Spock's Music From Outer Space.*

In 1977, Nimoy took on a different challenge when he was asked to take over the leading role in a Broadway play called "Equus." The play had been running for six years. Even though four famous actors had played the leading role before Nimoy, Leonard knew that he could bring something special to the part.

As he always does, Nimoy worked hard to prepare for his role. After rehearsing seven hours a day, he would go home and rehearse some more. His wife Sandi said that he even thrashed around in his sleep—rehearsing! Leonard played the role of a psychiatrist whose patient is a young stable boy who thinks God is a horse. To better understand the role

Leonard enjoyed learning about the relationships between horses and people to prepare for his "Equus" role.

and the ideas behind "Equus," he hired an animal behavior expert. Leonard spent many hours learning all about horses. Leonard feels that it is very important to really understand the roles he plays. "A character is like a plant," he says. "The richer the soil, the better it grows. One of the actor's jobs is to nourish his plants." Leonard was a hit in "Equus," and ticket sales for the show jumped.

From 1978 to 1981, Leonard combined his many talents in a one-man show called "Vincent"—a drama about the artist Vincent Van Gogh. He not only starred in the show, he wrote, directed, and co-produced it. "Vincent" went on tour all over the United States.

Once, when Leonard was in New York, he called the special events producer of the Guthrie Theater in Minneapolis, Minnesota, where he was scheduled to perform in "Vincent." He was concerned that the

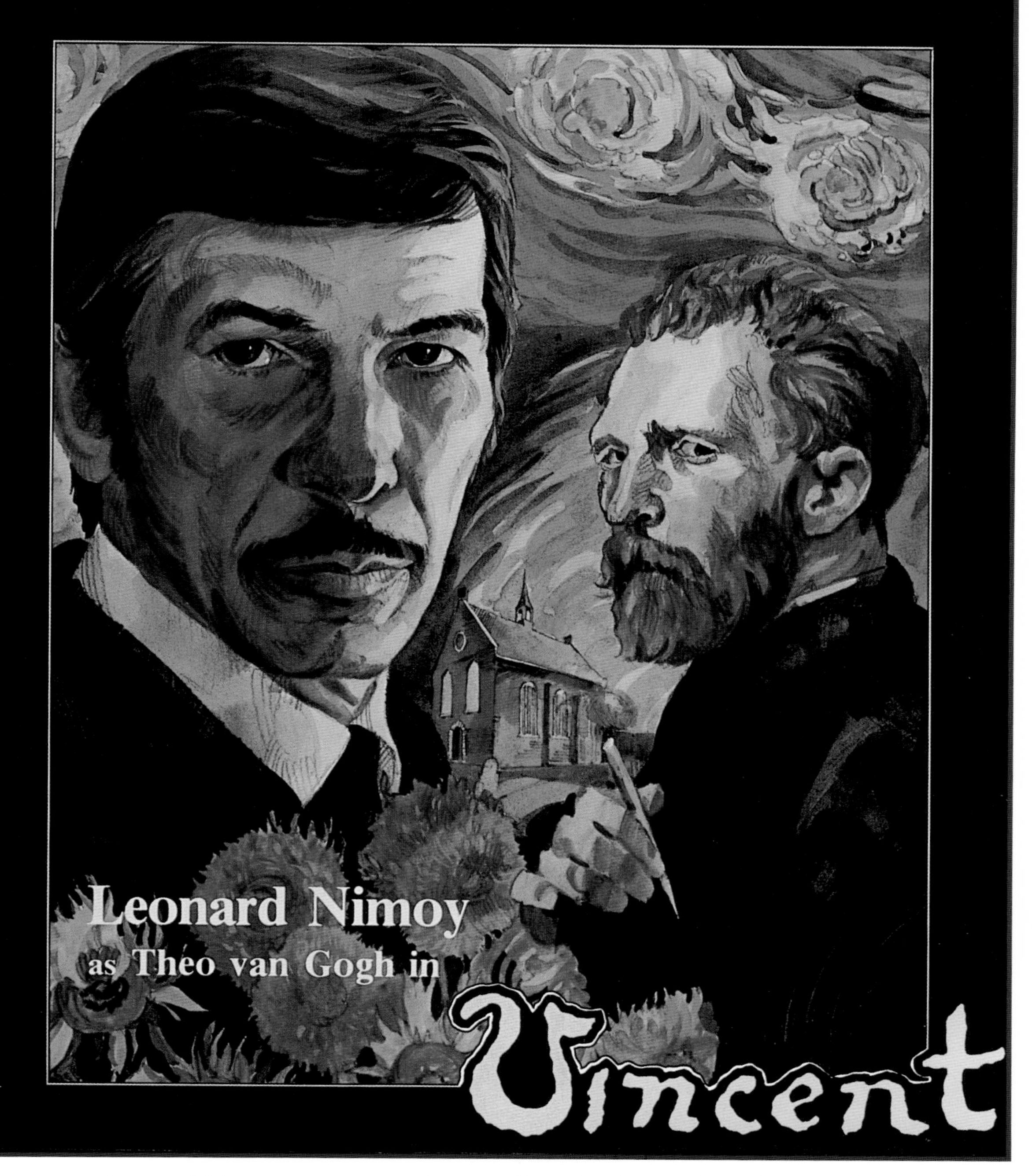

Leonard Nimoy, starring as Vincent Van Gogh's brother Theo, on this Guthrie Theater program cover, illustrated by Clif Hadfield.

stage might not be the right kind for his production, so he asked the producer, Dennis Babcock, if he could stop by and look at it on his way to California. Babcock was surprised by this unusual request, but was glad to oblige. "Leonard is unique as an artist," he says. "His dedication to quality in his work was extraordinary—he would always put in the extra yard for a good performance."

"Vincent" was a success at the Guthrie. "People would come to see 'Vincent' to see Mr. Spock," Babcock said, "but they left with an appreciation of Leonard Nimoy's talent as an actor and a deep understanding of a great artist—Vincent Van Gogh." Babcock and Nimoy decided to work together to take the show on tour to about fifty cities in the next three years, and later, to film the performance.

About this time, Leonard also served as host and narrator for the TV program "In Search Of. . . ." The program discussed myths, monsters, and ghosts. Hosting this show about the search for unusual things seemed perfect for the man who had played the half-alien Mr. Spock.

Though Leonard's achievements were many, his "Star Trek" days were not over. He would soon have a chance to play his most famous role.

Leonard Nimoy and William Shatner pose in their Star Trek II: The

5

Back to Star Trek

By the late 1970s, "Star Trek" was more popular than ever. The people who had watched it ten years earlier enjoyed the reruns. Many young people were now fans of "Star Trek."

With this is mind, Paramount decided to make a "Star Trek" movie. They contacted the original cast of the TV show because they wanted to use the actors that the fans knew and loved. At first, Leonard wasn't sure if he wanted to play Spock again. He didn't want his acting career to be limited to just playing that one character.

Leonard says that he "twisted and turned and discussed and thought and lay awake nights and argued with myself. . ." trying to decide whether or not to be in the new "Star Trek" movie. He finally decided to play Spock again. He didn't see how they could make the film without Spock. He didn't want to see another actor in the role he had made famous, either.

Star Trek: The Motion Picture cost about $45 million to make. In the movie, Star Fleet Command calls the crew members of the *Enterprise* back together for a special mission. They travel to Earth to save the planet from a mysterious and deadly space probe.

Like the TV show, the "Star Trek" movie series started slowly. Many of the critics didn't like the first "Star Trek" film, because it seemed to be mostly special effects. For the most part, the fans supported it—they were glad to see their "Star Trek" heroes again. The movie made money, and more "Star Trek" movies were planned.

The second "Star Trek" movie came out in 1982.

The Nimoy family, Julie, Leonard, Sandi, and Adam, gather at the 1982 Emmy Awards.

It was called *Star Trek II: The Wrath of Khan.* It focused more on people and less on special effects. In *Star Trek II*, Spock gives his life to save the crew of the *Enterprise* from the evil Khan, and his body is left behind on the planet Genesis. "Star Trek" fans wondered if this would be the end of Spock.

This mystery set the stage for the 1984 film, *Star Trek III: The Search for Spock.* At age fifty-three, Leonard got the idea to direct the film himself. He thought he could make the third "Star Trek" movie better than the first two. Paramount agreed that having Nimoy direct *Star Trek III* was a good idea. They knew he would do a good job, and also attract some good publicity for the movie.

Leonard looked forward to directing his fellow crew members. He understood their characters, and knew their strengths as actors. He was surprised when the cast members worried about having him as

Leonard Nimoy and William Shatner present the Academy Awards together in 1987.

their boss. They were used to working *with* him—they weren't sure that they would like working *for* him.

Things worked out well, though. Nimoy took his directing work as seriously as his acting. One day, Leonard was concentrating so hard on the filming that he didn't even notice a fire that was burning on a nearby set!

Hard work paid off, and *Star Trek III* became another box office hit. The first three "Star Trek" movies earned well over $100 million. As Spock would say, it seemed "logical" to keep on going.

Nimoy went on to direct *Star Trek IV: The Voyage Home*, which made its debut in late 1986. In the film, the "Star Trek" crew members once again return to Earth. This time, they need to save the world by taking a pair of humpback whales into the future.

Star Trek IV was by far the most popular of the

movies. It alone made over $100 million. The film drew a whole new group of fans, capturing the hearts of young and old viewers alike. This movie had more humor than the past "Star Trek" movies. One film critic said that Nimoy "knows exactly what audiences want to see," and called "Star Trek" a "treasured part of our culture."

Leonard said that he had "a great time" making *Star Trek IV*. He was proud of how it turned out. Though it was hard to direct the film and to star in it at the same time, he enjoyed his work.

"Star Trek" now seems to be more popular than ever—millions of fans watch the reruns and the movies. A "Star Trek" cartoon series ran from 1973 through 1975, and a new "Star Trek" TV series with a new crew made its debut in 1987.

"Star Trek" items such as games, cards, and models are a big business, too. Pocket Books releases six new "Star Trek" novels each year, and has sold at least ten million of these novels. "Star Trek" fans, known as "trekkies," still hold conventions all over the country where they watch reruns of "Star Trek," and trade books, buttons, and other items.

Leonard finds it hard to believe that "Star Trek" has been going on for more than twenty years. Playing Spock has opened many doors for him—the role made Leonard Nimoy rich and famous. Whatever projects he is involved in, the "Star Trek" character is never far away. When Leonard is spotted on the street, sometimes people can't think of his real name, but they always know that he played Spock. One person has even called him Leonard Spock!

On the whole, the twenty years of "Star Trek" have been good ones for Nimoy. But he has had some sad times as well. One such time came when he and his wife Sandi parted after more than thirty years of

Arching his eyebrow, Leonard Nimoy sports his Spock T-shirt.

marriage. One year later, in 1987, Leonard's father died. This came as a blow to Leonard, who was very close to his father.

Family still plays an important part in Leonard's life. He became a proud grandfather on February 20, 1985, when his daughter Julie had a baby boy named Alexander. Leonard enjoys spending time with his family, and keeps closely in touch with both Julie and his son Adam.

Today, Leonard Nimoy's career is more successful than ever. He directed Disney Pictures' movie *Three Men and a Baby*, and is being sought after to direct more movies. Best of all, he has the freedom to choose what projects he wants to work on. In many ways, "Star Trek" may have been just the beginning for Leonard Nimoy.

★ I N D E X ★

★ About the Author ★

John Micklos, Jr., from Newark, Delaware, is currently the editor of *Reading Today*, the bi-monthly membership newspaper of the International Reading Association. Also a free-lance writer, Micklos writes a monthly column on children's books for the *New Ark Post*, articles on reading education, and reading workbooks. He also has served as writer and contributing editor for *Delaware Today* magazine.